The Backyard Safari

Gary Richmond

WORD
kids!

Dallas • London • Sydney • Singapore

VIEW FROM THE ZOO STORIES are based on the real-life adventures of Gary Richmond, a veteran of the Los Angeles Zoo, minister, counselor, and camp nature speaker. Gary has three children and lives in Chino Hills, California, with his wife, Carol.

Library of Congress Cataloging-in-Publication Data

Richmond, Gary, 1944-
    The backyard safari / by Gary Richmond; illustrated
      by Bruce Day. p. cm.
    Summary: The author recounts a childhood experi-
ence with black widow spiders in which he learned the
importance of obeying his parents and God.
    ISBN 0-8499-0741-1: $7.99
    1. Obedience — Juvenile literature. 2. Children —
Religious life. [1. Obedience. 2. Christian life.] I. Day,
Bruce, ill.
II. Title.
BJ1459.R53 1990
241'.4 — dc20
                                     90-32207
                                     CIP
                                     AC

This book is dedicated to my son Gary, with whom
I have shared many of these kinds of adventures.

Hi, I'm Gary Richmond, and I'm a zoo keeper. As a zoo keeper, I've learned a lot about God's wonderful animals. At the same time, I've learned a lot about God.

The greatest lesson I ever learned from God's animals, though, was not learned in the zoo. It was learned in a mossy, moldy greenhouse; in the backyard of a lady I thought was a witch! I'd like to tell you about it.

Spring was almost over, and school was almost out for the summer. It was 1952, and I was eight years old. I was excited about having three whole months out of school. I could go barefooted and have a string of adventures.

One day Edgar Beasly from the Health Department knocked on our door. He told my mother about an epidemic of black widow spiders. He asked her to spray our yard for them. One little girl nearly died from a black widow bite! Mr. Beasly sounded really worried. Then he gave mom a booklet about black widows and left.

Mom looked through the booklet. The longer she looked, the bigger her frown became. Then she handed me the booklet. She said, "Gary, I'd better not catch you even walking by a black widow spider web. If you do, I'll spank your back side shiny. Do you understand me, young man?"

I said yes and started looking at the booklet. It was neat! On the cover was the picture of a mean-looking female black widow. A red hourglass spot was on her black, shiny stomach. The booklet said she lived in a funny-shaped web. Black widows were usually found in dark places like garages, wood piles and under cabinets.

It said that a black widow bite might cause terrible things to happen. The person's skin might swell up. Or it might turn a funny color around the bite. The person might be sick at his stomach. Or he might have a bad headache. He might have a hard time breathing. Or his eyes might go all blurry. It said that children could even die from the bite!

Mom had just given me the greatest idea of my life: a black widow safari right in my own backyard! I couldn't wait to tell my best friend, Doug.

"Look, Doug," I said, "my folks will be gone Saturday for about three hours. That's enough time to catch ten black widow spiders. We'll take them down to our school. And we'll dump them on that big red ant hill. It will be great! The red ants will come running out to protect their hill. Then there will be a big, scary fight. The red ants will win. And we'll have helped to fight black widows."

"What if we get bit?" asked Doug.

"We're not going to let those child-killers get us. We'll be really careful. Hey, you're not going to chicken out on me, are you?"

"Well, no," Doug said slowly.

I made Doug do the bloodbrother handshake. He had to promise not to tell anyone about our safari. He shook, knowing that if he told his teeth and hair would fall out.

I found an old peanut butter jar. We poked holes in its lid so the spiders could breathe. We chose a two-foot stick for catching spiders. Then we hid our safari gear behind the garage until Saturday.

As soon as my parents left to go shopping, I ran to Doug's house. He was waiting for me in his front yard. We grabbed our gear and headed for my backyard. I had already found several webs. On the way we met our friend Eric. He was coming over to play. We finally decided we'd have to let Eric go on the safari, too. But we made him take an even more serious oath than Doug. Eric didn't keep secrets very well.

Eric really wanted to go; so, he took this oath: "I promise never to tell about the black widow safari. If I do the Devil will make my mother's hair fall out." He didn't really want to say the part about his mom and the Devil, but he did.

We walked down our long driveway. And we ran right into my twelve-year-old brother, Steve. Before we could stop him, Eric said, "Guess what, Steve? We're going on a safari to catch black widow spiders. We're going to dump them on a red ant hill. Isn't that neat?"

Steve said the words we hated most: "You guys are too young to do that!" But he did think it sounded like a great idea. So, he offered to catch the spiders for us. If we were good, he would let us hold the jar.

We followed Steve to the backyard. I shook my fist at Eric. I said, "I'm never telling you another secret. I hope you're thinking about what you just did to your mother."

Eric tried to picture his mother bald. He wondered if she would know that it was his fault. I sadly handed the catching stick to Steve. Then Doug handed the peanut butter jar to me.

It only took a minute to find the first spider behind our tool shed. Her web was full of dried bodies — three moths and two flies. She was one scary-looking spider.

We all huddled behind Steve to watch him catch her. He got her on the stick. Then he told me to open the jar. With trembling hands I opened the jar. With a tap of the stick the first prisoner was trapped. She was a medium-sized spider. And she was not happy about being caught. She looked just like the spider on the booklet cover. When I lifted the jar we could see the bright red hourglass spot on her stomach.

As the jar began filling up, my job became more difficult. The fifth spider attached a web to the jar lid. When I opened the jar for the sixth spider, I pulled the creepy web across my hand. I shivered and quickly put the lid back on.

We had caught eight ugly-looking spiders. We couldn't find any more in our yard. We couldn't think where else to look. Then Eric, who had been quietly watching spoke up. "I bet the evil queen of the black widow spiders lives in Mrs. Brown's greenhouse."

Now, Mrs. Brown lived next door to Doug. All the kids in our neighborhood were afraid of her. She didn't like small children. She would even call the police if they set foot in her yard. Some of us thought she was a witch. We thought she could cast spells that could keep us under her power...and stuff like that.

Suddenly, the safari became exciting again. It was such a great idea that Eric was forgiven for breaking the oath. He was glad. He said he couldn't get used to the idea of his mom being bald.

We decided to sneak into Mrs. Brown yard from Doug's backyard. Her greenhouse was in the very back of her yard. We peaked over Doug's fence into the jungle of her yard. We decided she was not outside. One at a time we dropped over the fence into enemy territory. Then we slipped silently into the greenhouse.

It was damp and dark, musty and moldy — a perfect place for black widows. We all thought Mrs. Brown would jump out and grab us at any minute; so, we had Eric stand guard.

Under the garden bench was a five-gallon red clay pot. It was turned upside down on three red bricks. Steve and Doug turned it over slowly and carefully. We gasped at what we saw. At the bottom of the pot was a huge black widow. She was the biggest spider we had ever seen! She was fat

and full of poison. She was protecting her silky white sac of eggs. And she was not afraid of Steve's stick.

Finally, Steve got the deadly giant on the stick. He told me to open the jar. I shook the jar until I could count the other eight spiders. Carefully, I turned the lid and took it off the jar. My hands were trembling. Steve brought the stick to the mouth of the jar. He was just about to drop her in the jar.

Suddenly, she made a leap for it! She landed right between my feet. I backed away quickly. But during the excitement I forgot to put the lid back on the jar. I was too busy watching the evil one at my feet.

My eyes were glued to Steve and that queen spider. I didn't see a medium-sized black widow crawling out of the jar. It crept onto the back of my hand. Slowly I had an eerie feeling. I stared in terror at the little killer. It was taking a morning stroll on my hand!

I let the jar slip through my fingers. Black widows began to run everywhere. It didn't matter anymore. The safari game was over. I was so scared I couldn't say real words. But I got out a pretty good "yaaaaaAAAAAA!"

Steve looked at me, and he was scared, too. I was sure I was going to die — not like in cowboys and indians where you get up again. This was real dying where everything goes dark...for good.

It took all my strength to keep from fainting. I could feel every soft footstep of that deadly spider. I stayed perfectly still. I was praying she wouldn't bite me. I begged Steve with tears in my eyes to please get the spider off my hand. He moved his index finger in a flicking position. He was within an inch of the killer. I held my breath. And I

wanted to close my eyes. But I was afraid it would be for the last time.

The black widow stopped to look at Steve's threatening finger. When she did, Steve flicked with all his might. The spider went flying, and I've never been more relieved in my life.

We all went running out of that death trap. We ran through the jungle and scrambled back over the fence into Doug's yard. We lay on the ground panting for several minutes. That was close! Too close! And, you know, I've never gone spider hunting again.

That black widow safari taught me an important lesson: I should obey the rules my parents give me — they're for my own good. My mom told me to stay away from black widow spiders. She knew they could kill me. It wasn't because she didn't want me to have any fun. She loves me, see?

Sometimes I think about God like that, too. He gave us some rules to live by in the Bible. He gave them to us so we can have a happy life and because he loves us. He knows that life is like a safari into the jungle. There are dangerous traps we should avoid. I, for one, have learned to listen to what God says. How about you?